Baby Animals

PUPPY

Angela Royston

Chrysalis Children's Books

First published in the UK in 2004 by

Chrysalis Children's Books
An imprint of Chrysalis Books Group PLC,
The Chrysalis Building, Bramley Road, London W10 6SP

ISBN 1 84458 084 9

British Library Cataloguing in Publication Data for this book is available from the British Library.

Editorial Manager: Joyce Bentley
Editor: Clare Lewis

Produced by Bender Richardson White
Project Editor: Lionel Bender
Designer: Ben White
Production: Kim Richardson
Picture Researcher: Cathy Stastny
Cover Make-up: Mike Pilley, Radius

Printed in China

10 9 8 7 6 5 4 3 2 1

Words in **bold** can be found in New words on page 31.

> **NOTE**
> In this book, we have used photographs of different types of puppies and adult dogs. Each type has fur of a certain colour and pattern.

Picture credits
Chrysalis Books/Jane Burton: 22, 24.
Corbis Images Inc: Ariel Skelley 27.
Ecoscene: Sally Morgan 7, 9, 20; Peter Cairns 28.
Natural History Photo Agency: Gerard Lacz 4; Yves Lanceau 6, 17; Ernie Janes 11; Joe Blossom 15; David Tomlinson 18.
Oxford Scientific Films: Lon E Lauber 21.
Rex Features Ltd: Paul Brown 14; Steve Lake 23.
RSPCA Photolibrary: Cheryl A Ertelt, cover, 13, 19; E A Janes 1, 5, 8, 10, 12; Andrew Forsyth 2, 25; Angela Hampton 16, 26, 29.

Contents

Newly born

This little puppy has just been born. His **fur** is all wet.

The mother dog licks the puppy until his fur is dry and fluffy.

First few hours

The mother dog has given birth to three puppies. She is very proud of her **litter**!

The puppies cannot see or hear yet. Their eyes are shut even when they are awake.

Feeding

The puppy is hungry. He smells his mother's milk and soon starts to feed.

All the puppies are feeding.
They push each other to get
to their mother's **teats**.

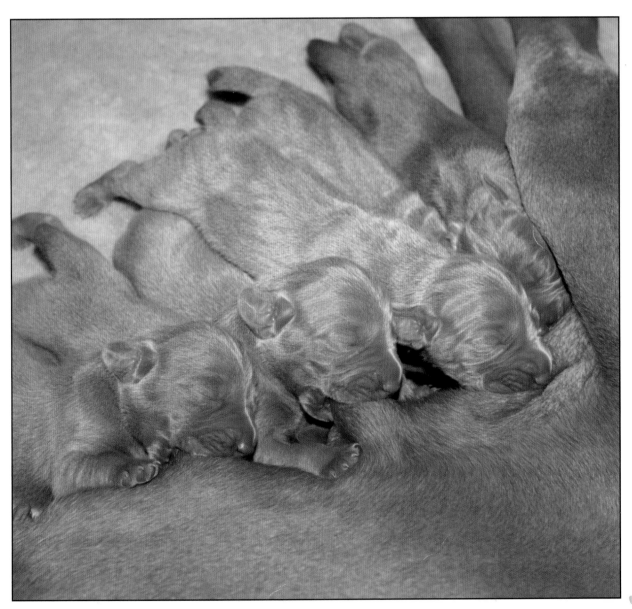

Ten days old

The puppies open their eyes for the first time. Everything looks blurred.

The puppies can hear now, too. They hear each other **breathing** as they crawl around.

Two weeks old

The puppies spend more time awake now. They crawl and climb and start to **explore**.

Their legs are still weak and **wobbly**. Trying to stand, walk and climb soon tires them out.

Four weeks old

The puppies are very **curious**. They sniff everything to find out what it smells like.

If one of them finds an interesting smell, he follows it with his nose.

Becoming bolder

Puppies love to play. They chase anything that moves, even a wiggling puppy's tail!

The mother watches over all the puppies. If one **strays** too far, she calls it back.

Going outside

The puppies are old enough to go outside now. There are many new smells out here!

They sniff the grass, the soil
and the plants. They run around
and play with one another.

Eight weeks old

These puppies are exploring and play-fighting.

They **growl** and **yap**, but they do not hurt each other. They are finding out which of them is stronger.

Solid food

The puppies no longer feed on their mother's milk. They eat special dog food instead.

Sometimes they are given a dog biscuit or dog chew for a treat.

Three months old

Each puppy is given a new **lead**. This puppy is going out for its first walk.

The lead stops the puppy from running off or going on to the road.

Six months old

The puppies
have grown
bigger and
have learnt
to do what
they are told.

This puppy comes when his name is called and he sits when his **owner** says, 'Sit!'

Grown up

By 12 months, puppies are fully grown. When they **bark**, they make a loud, deep sound.

Most of the puppies now live with new owners, who look after them.

Quiz

1 How many puppies did the mother dog have?

2 How old are puppies when they first open their eyes?

3 What food do puppies like to eat as treats?

4 Why do puppies play-fight?

5 At what age do puppies learn to do what they are told by their owner?

6 Why should puppies be kept on leads when they are outdoors?

7 What sounds do puppies make?

8 How old are puppies when they are fully grown?

The answers are all in this book!

New words

bark noise made by a dog.

breathing taking air into the body and pushing it out again.

curious wanting to find out about something.

explore to find out for oneself.

fur thick hair that covers an animal's body.

growl warning noise made by a dog, puppy and some other animals.

lead a long piece of fabric or leather that goes round a puppy or dog's neck.

litter a group of puppies born at the same time.

owner person who owns something, such as a dog.

stray to wander off on one's own, out of sight.

teat part of a mother's body from which her babies suck milk.

wobbly shaky, unsteady.

yap high-pitched bark made by a puppy or a small dog.

Index